Why We Live
in the Dark Ages

for Sarah, with gratitude — enjoy (whether you're the little sports or the big sports)!

4/7/18

Why We Live in the Dark Ages

Megan Levad

TAVERN BOOKS

PORTLAND

Cover art: Cecilia Yang, *Bunsen Burner,* 2014. Ink drawing.
Copyright © Cecilia Yang. Courtesy of the artist.

Levad, Megan, 1978-

ISBN-13: 978-1-935635-41-3 (paperback)
ISBN-13: 978-1-935635-42-0 (hardcover)

LCCN: 2014958442

FIRST EDITION

98765432 First Printing

This book was selected through the 2013-2014 Wrolstad Contemporary Poetry Series,
an annual Tavern Books program highlighting the work of young female poets.

TAVERN BOOKS
Union Station
800 NW 6th Avenue #255
Portland, Oregon 97209
www.tavernbooks.com

Index

For Paul

Why We Live
in the Dark Ages

I know that I am mortal by nature and ephemeral, but when I trace at my pleasure the windings to and fro of the heavenly bodies, I no longer touch earth with my feet. I stand in the presence of Zeus himself and take my fill of ambrosia.

—Claudius Ptolemy, *Almagest*

Monotremes

Mammals were just starting up when Australia broke off, um, rifted
separated from Pangea and drifted away to the South Seas. Australia.
The Antipodes. All their love stories are freaking tragic. Have you ever
seen *Walkabout?* Good god. But when mammals started up they were just
secreting sweat-milk and their young were licking it off their bodies and
then they moved, they sailed off to Australia and they stayed that way
or at least at least some of them did. And the rest developed breasts.
Which means that most well maybe not most but a lot, a lot of men have
some deeply ambivalent feelings about women. Like they're going to make
them feel terrible any second. It's humiliating to desire your mother
so much. But she's your food. You're eating your mother's sweat
for maybe, for some people, the first two years of your life, sometimes
three, four, I read about a five-year-old in *The New York Times* who was
nursing but it was an essay by his father who admitted to some jealousy
there's this part where, where he describes the boy, his son nursing on a
blanket in Central Park and he's lying down and he's stretched out long
and you get the sense of the father, his father maybe having a, a kind of
rival in the lad. And it sounds like maybe that boy was maybe a little bit of a
pawn in his parents' marriage game. I mean if you're nursing until five then
you also probably, maybe that means you, you literally put your child
between you and its father when you sleep so maybe it is also a good excuse
not to have boring sex with your boring husband anymore, or maybe you
just find him kind of gross compared to a soft little hairless baby who
smells all fresh, and men, grown-ups, they're rough and hairy and

their toenail fungus and their gum disease and their belly-button lint maybe
all seems kind of sad and reminds us of death. People need to chill out
about back hair and cellulite. They're just secondary sex characteristics.
Like breasts. Which are for feeding the young. But not all mammals
have breasts, some of them, like the Australian ones, just secrete their milk
which is sweat, it, it comes from a modified sweat gland I mean breasts are
modified sweat glands. They secrete it. Secretly it pools in sort of, um
divots these um, shallow inverted places on their chests and bellies, like
rudimentary nipple sites maybe. The young lap it up. So they must
have divots. Lapping, lapping requires some kind of dish
or something, if there's no accumulation of liquid it would be licking, right?
So echidnas and platypuses and maybe that's it, only Australian animals
have milk but no nipples, no breasts. But breasts, modified edible-sweat
glands, they started way way way earlier than you, than you might think
and maybe even some reptiles had them but those reptiles aren't around
anymore so we think of them as just a mammal thing, as an inherent
mammalian characteristic, but mammary glands or like the monotremes
the patches for licking the monotremes have, those are really really really old
like Pennsylvanian. William Penn. Who would've thought. He gets an era
named after him. And he was a, a Quaker. Like Nixon and Hoover, the two
worst presidents of America. So, there were these, these sweaty hair follicles
that started to, to um, concentrate in patches like those shadows, those
sort of ghost balls that are left after you neuter a cat, those patches helped
feed the eggs when the monotremes were setting nests and the sweat-milk

the milk-sweat would drip down on the soft-shelled eggs and they would get nutrition until the milk-sweat got so good and the monotremes got so good at dripping it that their babies didn't need to be in eggs didn't need to incubate very long at all and they started to just come out and lick up milk-sweat from inside the pouch, like kangaroos or koalas and they got a lot cuter or at least we think they're cuter. I have no idea about opossums though. No idea. How they got to America. And why they're so gross.

Bullying

Maybe it feels new now because kids do it with the phone. I don't know.
I don't want to sound like a like a, Back in my day, but this is not
a new thing. Witch hunts. Shunnings. Marcia, Marcia, Marcia.
Cheerleaders. But in the movies, even cheerleader movies, everyone loves
the bad girl I mean everyone watching it knows she's not bad and we're
supposed to the audience is supposed to root for her. So it's not like we don't
know. Everyone loves the weird hot girl who takes dares and develops early
and has a different-colored eye which, by the way, if you have a different-
color eye it means you ate your twin, I mean you, you absorbed your twin
in, in the womb, you would have been twins, like before you were a zygote
you could have, but inside your mother your cells that turned into you
those cells absorbed the cells of your possible, your potential twin. Except
the eye. Cannibals. In another time those people would be worshipped or
sacrificed. I guess they still are. Bullying is kind of both. All that focus on
the power, the role of, I mean everyone just focused on how one person
fits into or doesn't fit into the community. It's real old-time stuff.

Homeopathy

Nanostructures. Yes. If you say something is nano then everyone A knows it's tiny and B thinks you're smart. Because you know about this thing that's too small to be seen with the naked eye. Nanostructures are in homeopathy which, which believes, is the belief in, is the medical practice if, if you can call it that, the scientific community thinks it's bunk snake oil but if you believe in it, in homeopathy, you believe that you can put a little bit of something that's making you sick or something that would give you the same symptoms as the illness you're having, you can put a very very tiny little bit of it in a mixture of, of water and I think of some alcohol and if you shake it in a certain way, it's a patented kind of shaking, sort of like the Epley Maneuver, which is a way that the doctors, real doctors white coat doctors in hospitals will move you around, move your head and body around in such a way that the crystals in your ears get back into place. Fit back into place. If you have vertigo. Anyway. If you are anxious and irritable maybe your homeopath will put a little coffee, or caffeine really, because coffee makes people anxious and irritable, so they will put a little bit in this water and alcohol solution and shake it in a certain way and the molecular structures will be left behind after it's all dissolved in. They will be nanostructures. I think so your body can absorb them more easily? But the problem is that if the amount is too tiny then your body probably won't notice at all especially since you have to take these little pills or drink these tinctures. So scientists don't think it works. But it's sort of what Ritalin is based on, and also allergy shots, and homeopaths say there are studies that show it works even if they can't really explain it. That sounds like bullshit. But that also sounds like everything that's supposed to be natural, it's just natural, and that's it! If you don't agree you're unnatural. It's a tautology. You can't blame people though, because if you think about it, so homeopathy was started two hundred years ago by a German doctor and even just two hundred years ago we knew the earth went around the sun and wasn't flat and how gravity works and that we're made of cells, but people were still, still getting their blood let bleeding, using leeches, well, we're still using leeches, but they were taking arsenic and all kinds of things that sound barbaric now. So maybe homeopathy worked because it was doing nothing. First, do no harm. It's based on Hippocrates, the homeopathy, the idea of like defeats like fight fire with fire. Hippocrates was also the one who said first do no harm. Which seems obvious but if you have to differentiate, I mean if you are making doctoring, being a physician or pharmacist, apothecary, if you're making that a special job, a specialization in your civilization, then you need to make sure they're not just killing the sick people because anyone can do that. So then there were witches and herbalists and the old lady you would go to if you were pregnant and didn't want to be or if you weren't pregnant and wanted to be and she would give you some herbs to fix you up. And then people didn't like being reminded of the old knowledge and paganism so they had the witch trials. Also it was a good way to, good way to get rid of your wife's girlfriend or the woman you had an affair with or something. Or just fewer mouths to feed in Salem. But the people two hundred years from now might think that we're barbaric barbarous people, did you know that the barbarians got called that because the Romans thought that's how they talked, how their language sounded barbarbarbar? In two hundred years though, they might look at how we treat cancer and say, Wow. They just poisoned people until the part that wasn't their original body, the cancerous growths, the extra cells rampaging, they poisoned them until the cancer died. But hopefully the person didn't. Like tying off your belly button. So if you get cancer you might want to try homeopathy because at least it's very very weak poison. First, do no harm.

Polio

Polio is one of the one of the diseases that we, we humans have been able to almost totally prevent. Almost wipe out. Well, not wipe out because it's still here, vaccines don't exterminate viruses they just keep people from getting sick from them or spreading them more. But they only have polio in Nigeria and Afghanistan and Pakistan now. If I were a conspiracy person. Of course sometimes there's an outbreak, like in Syria there was an outbreak of polio recently I mean in the recent teens, '10s, I think an outbreak among, I want to say Armenian Syrians. And Armenia I think sent a bunch of polio vaccine to Syria but I don't know how people got it. I think that happened. Someone should make a movie about that if it did happen. Like a quiet war movie like we love because if you're anti-war you can still hate the bad guys but you don't have to feel guilty about their heads exploding, and you don't have to, have to hear the people around you get all excited about the exploding heads. You don't have to sit there and think, How gauche, and then feel like a jerk. So polio is only in primates and it's almost gone, but now that some, some parents think vaccines give their kids autism even though that's been disproved over and over, or maybe they just want their kids to be pure, this is a very Rousseuvian moment we're in you know, toxins, cleansing, go back to the land and make belts or rare charcuteries, they want their kids pure. No intervention. Intervention like in war. Everyone is at war with nature, really, nature is as hostile as it gets. Like it really I mean literally does not care if you live or die. Actually maybe it wants you to die so I guess it does care. Anyway, I think we have these bad feelings about killing inside ourselves and those are meant to be there to make sure we don't say, Oh hi saber-toothed tiger! But we feel bad about them because we're super-civilized now and so we've repressed those feelings, those killing feelings, in order to make cities and art. See Freud. So maybe now we're so civilized we don't even want to believe that we need to be hostile to viruses. We're going to sit around and just not take all these great medicines we invented. In Africa some people think that the polio vaccine sterilizes you. And probably sometimes the people giving the polio vaccine actually do sterilize people too, probably even without consent because that's not uncommon. And some people also think HIV came from the polio vaccine, from the inoculations in the Belgian colonies the Congo and Rwanda and, and I can't remember the other one. Wow Belgium never gets shit for how badly they fucked up their colonies. Anyway, the rhesus monkey kidneys used to make or test the polio vaccine they did carry some other disease like non-Hodgkins lymphoma, and a lot of people were exposed in the US and then later the US stopped using the monkey kidneys, by the early '60s, but the Soviet Union and China and a lot of African countries were still getting the monkey vaccine so who knows.

Nanobots

All of the nanobots? Or just the nanobots in the bloodstream? You know the new immune system. Nanobots are really small tiny robots and, and um basically, if you were to get cancer or something where your body doesn't naturally respond they would inject the nanobots, oh, they're self-replicating of course, so the nanobots are self-replicating so when they're in your bloodstream say you'd only have to inject like two, I guess only one it's not like they're mating or anything. So the one would be in the bloodstream and it just starts reproducing itself and it's programmed to attack the cancer or other ailment. Also if your limb gets cut off or something it will rebuild your bones using your body's tissue or whatever. It will rebuild. They don't exist yet. They're working on it.

Fur

There were these foxes on a fur farm and these furriers who, who got bored
or something, I don't know, they were in Russia, the Soviet Union, so maybe
they were shipped off from their families in Ukraine and Lithuania and I
don't know but they started to tame the foxes, domesticate them, well they
were technically um, um, domesticated animals already I guess
if they were being farmed for their fur which is cruel but would you
rather just be going along with your little happy fox life, Oh, I like chicken
I like fish I don't have to eat off a dish tra la la la la and then snap! it's over
you die instantly? Or live in a home with other foxes and just get cat food
or dog food or whatever foxes get, probably dead horse, leftover horse meat
before the bones get turned into glue or gelatin or whatever.
When you put it that way. Or you don't even get to live in the forest and
the fields or in a barn but have to live in a subdivision or behind a strip mall.
George Saunders wrote about it. In kind of a pidgin English like
the fox is writing it himself which is sort of nice and endearing but also
just silly, but maybe silly, silliness makes you think, think about something
differently, like from the side more. Because you're loosened, your mind
is loosened up. Also Roald Dahl did. God I loved that book! And probably
you don't, you don't die instantly I mean immediately in a trap, probably
you end up trying to chew your leg off and dying of dehydration. Man.
And I'm not even anti-fur. Jesus. Trapping. And fur is beautiful you know
you know how you can tell when somebody's coat or just hood trim, the
trim, the trim on the hood of their coat like a nimbus, when that, that's real
because it all moves, the individual hairs move and bounce like, well, like

27

hair? Apparently that's the hardest thing to do in CGI. So if you see
a cartoon, an animated movie with lots of hair shots, that's, they're, they're
showing off how good their animators are. And not wasting all that time.
Money. So the Russian fur farmers were looking for ways to pass the time so
they started taming foxes, that is, I don't know, they would hand-feed them
maybe or they would just try to touch them? Taming equals touching
for some reason. But the point is that in just a few fox generations
the babies were born tame. They just weren't born with that fear of humans.
Naturally. They were naturally open to, friendly to people. They would be
born seeing people as a friend and caretaker. Also their ears fell down
they drooped like dogs' ears, and they started to wag their tails.

Genetic Engineering

What is that called, human—where you're trying to, engineering genetics. Where basically your job is to manipulate genes in order to make, when you screw with life and change animals' chemistry so they, I don't know what is that called? Genetic engineering! So there was a guy who, one of these genetic engineers who wanted to use cows and manipulate their genes so they could be a host for organs for humans, so by modifying their genes you could grow, I don't know, human kidneys in them and make their blood human.

Great Men of Science: Mendeleev

Well Mendeleev as you know discovered, he, he made the periodic table.
He also did experiments with peas to prove that genes come from
both parents, not just the father. No. That was Mendel. Just Mendel. But
I think they lived at the same time. Well so, the way he, the way Mendeleev
came up with the periodic table was, well first the ancients used to think
about the elements as wind fire and water. I was going to say ground but
I don't think that was one. So basically what happened with that was that
in the 18th century they started dividing those elements further, like
they discovered that the wind was made of gases and the ground could be
divided into different properties and they kept going further and further
until they discovered atoms. And they discovered atoms were different
and could do different things like some could fuse easily with other atoms.
So Mendeleev found that if you ordered the gases in such a way that they
would start lightest and go to heaviest and if you did that that pattern
would keep happening but you would also have elements that would deviate
from it but they would deviate in a way that would create another pattern.
Because basically chemistry is the study of why different elements are
attracted to each other or why they are disgusted by each other.

Fractions

Fractions. You just cut shit up. You know divide things. In many pieces.
And then you talk about the whole and its parts. And how they relate
to one another.

Great Men of Science: Beethoven

Apparently Beethoven was not very good at math especially when it came to accounting, and his entire life he always thought himself broke. And as a result throughout his life he kept opening new accounts to put the latest amount of money that he received for a commission into this account because he thought through his poor accounting skills that he had no more money left in the other accounts. So he would just open, so he kept, so he kept opening new accounts. Anyway when Beethoven died he died thinking that he was poor but in actuality he was very wealthy because of all of the money in all of these accounts that had not been drained were many and plentiful and helped support his nephew Karl. So I guess it's a myth that all musicians are good at math. Because the best ones aren't!

Gravity

Oh I don't know anything about gravity. I can't explain that.

Why We Live in the Dark Ages

Oh the Dark Ages. Let me tell you about the Dark Ages. Okay. Oh. I was reading this lecture by Jacques Barzun. B-a-r-z-u-n. B-a-r-z-u-n. Who is a great culture historian. Art historian. Anyway the lecture was called, uh "The Use and Abuse of Art." And there's a section in this lecture where he talks about the Dark Ages. And how it relates to our own time. A very popular subject. And he made a very interesting point. That the reason why no, no a very interesting point that in the Dark Ages the people of this time period were, were smart people essentially. They had art they had, uh, you know I don't know, interesting conversation, I don't know, they were, they were consumers they were functioning people but the reason why we refer to it as the Dark Ages is because not much, is basically because the populace of, we view them as being sort of dumb and, uh, from our standpoint because they weren't literate in the Latin which was the language everything was being written in for like, the intellectuals and, uh, all this intellectual thought was going on and was controlled largely by the Church. And he makes a comparison to our own time where our populace is, you know we may be literate and, um, producing art and doing all these sorts of things but the power within our society is in science and that, most of us sort of everyday people don't really understand science very well and uh like Latin to the Church sort of like abstract or, or any sort of scientific thought isn't common, isn't common language among our society at all and all the power is held with scientists or this very select group of people in the scientific community.

Prison

It's only a little while really a rather new thing actually that prison is
the punishment. The punishment itself. Instead of being, being jail, or
you could say we only had jails at least in the West there were only jails, no
prisons, until the Renaissance really the Enlightenment. Not until there
were juries, a jury of your peers or probably not your peers but of people
who the mayor or whoever was in charge in your village or city—who was
in charge in 17th-century London? The Queen? Did they have a prime
minister by then? I think so. Anyway it doesn't matter this is, usually they
juries were usually civic affairs. So the jury would find a thief, say
Not guilty or Innocent, I think Not guilty is a particularly American
thing because we have to we have the burden of proof. But they would
these jurors wouldn't want to hang or drown or cut up a thief because
understandably that was kind of extreme. Also because of the Reformation
people believed in um, um, reform. So the jail where people, usually poor
people, waited for trial became the punishment. That concept. And also it
was based on the work house or the poor house where you would be sent
if you were stealing or maybe selling illegal goods like maybe you aren't
allowed to sell a certain color silk or a certain kind of spice without a permit
or a duty, is that where those, where duties come from? Oh, the duty-free
shop. Last time I was in one someone dropped a huge bottle of perfume
I think Flowerbomb or I don't know, Marc Jacobs, but it was amazing.
She was probably drunk. What's sadder than an airport bar? Also the
poor could get sent to prison if they were drunk and rowdy. Or if you
were begging when you had your legs to work. Which could maybe be a

way of forcing people to accept low wages. This was in the beginnings of
capitalism. Post-Plague. And they would teach you, the guards I guess, or
maybe nuns would teach you to work in the poor house. Or really
you would just work for free. Maybe they were the first factories.
The beginnings of the Industrial Revolution. Also that would keep
the unemployment rate down for sure and so there must have been
prime ministers because queens aren't elected. And then the Quakers
and the Dutch started to really care about the prisons and they made them
separate the men and women and I think they made things better
for people who were sent to Australia though maybe getting sent to
Australia was kind of cool and romantic or at least you could feel like
things are going to be really really different from now on. Also Jeremy
Bentham. I remember this from Foucault who also says that this all comes
from the Plague, he, Jeremy Bentham invented the panopticon so one guard
could watch a lot of prisoners at once. In case someone was sick, or
in trouble. They could help them out. And from that we get film theory.

The French Revolution

Javert. Javert's power issues ruin that whole story. The French Revolution's actually about real structural, political problems, like how countries were being formed and overthrowing the old kings and queens and courts and all the petit fours and gigantic wigs were ridiculous and we needed square, stable republics instead of kingdoms. Short hair, brown clothes. Or we were going, I mean the Western European countries, not we but America sort of acts like it's Western Europe, part of it, anyway, an annex. I guess Canada really is, so that makes sense, sort of. I mean anyway that the West wasn't going to be able to compete with China and Persia and Arabia if they didn't get it together and quit wasting money on the royal families. Except those countries all had royal families too. But they also had more peasants. That Stalin joke, you underestimate how many people live in my country and how little I care about their lives. But that's boring. I mean for a show. So *Les Miserables* and I don't mean Victor Hugo it's not his fault, *Les Miz*—barf—turns it into a spaghetti Western, but not Italian, so no moody horizons or, and with terrible music-box twaddle instead of "How the West Was Won." And then Bill Clinton uses it in his campaign and we all think that he's a progressive. "Do You Hear the People Sing?" Also that Wings song, was it "We Built This City"? Maybe he meant it to refer to Augustine. St. Augustine. Who also had some trouble with women.

Fashion

People don't think about this very often but when the Louisiana, when Alexander Hamilton, no, Madison, when James Madison went to France to buy, broker the Louisiana Purchase, he was the Secretary of State for Thomas Jefferson and France was broke because of the revolution, well actually the kings probably broke them and then Napoleon's wars. So Napoleon, knowing that he couldn't afford to take over all of Europe and I think Northern Africa, he had to sell the French land in America. It wasn't the US yet. All those trappers. And their indigenous wives who maybe didn't want to be their wives. Maybe were sold to them. Or maybe the indigenous women liked the new guys. There is something to be said for novelty. Or maybe the trappers didn't even seem novel, after all the French were all along the Great Lakes and the Mississippi and the Missouri for hundreds of years. Since the 1500s. Since Shakespeare. Actually before Shakespeare. So Napoleon needs money to finish his world domination, partly because he's running out of cannon fodder, by which I mean people. Who he knew were just going to die. But he didn't care. Because of the glory of France. Which he needed to get back after the revolution. To show that an emperor was even better than a king. Also Josephine was born to be an empress and I love this, she was Creole from Martinique, and she is the great-great-great-great-great-, who knows grandmother of the Danish and the Swedish and the Norwegian and the Belgian royalty. So the Scandinavian royalty is Creole. Which is nice because those countries are so racist. We like to think of them as just perfect little social democracies but how hard is it to be a socialist when you have a ton of natural resources and you're related to everyone in your country? Anyway that's from her, from Josephine's first marriage, but her husband's head was chopped off in the guillotine and she was put in prison. And then she married Napoleon and he was crazy about her, he once sent her a letter that said he'd be home in three days, don't wash. That's good hot love. But she didn't have a baby with him so he got a new young wife from Austria, one like Marie Antoinette. Who did not have a hot marriage at all, but that was probably because they were only fourteen and fifteen and they didn't know what to do. Josephine had been married before. So Napoleon was broke and when he sold the Louisiana Purchase to James Madison for America, Dolly Madison came along to see France and she and Josephine hit it off and Dolly came back with Empire dresses. Cleavage. Not insane giant wigs full of lice. Sexy but plain. Milkmaid.

Great Men of Science: Anne Sexton

So Anne Sexton was born in 1928 to a, an upper middle-class family
mostly upper. She was a, a troubled child, kind of a floozy, she liked
the attention of men, men's attention. Her self-esteem really rested in men
how men viewed her which is problematic as anyone would, well anyway
she one night decided she was going to elope with this guy named Kato, or
that was her pet name for him, so they elope and she leaves this note
to her parents saying don't be mad we're really in love we had to do this.
She was probably sixteen or eighteen at that point so she could do it
without consent. And I think her parents were pretty angry, she didn't get
along with them. So after the drama or the dramatics of getting married
wear down she realizes that she really doesn't have anything else to do
except clean house, keep a tidy house and uh, domestic things. So she, she
has her first mental breakdown. She had her first kid, after she had her child
Linda she tried to kill herself and then she was put in a mental hospital. She
didn't really have anything to live for, she didn't want to identify herself as
just a mother and she didn't want to just be a loving wife because, well
uh, she was crazy but I wouldn't want to do that either. So her psychiatrist
tells her to start writing poetry because she had some, a bit of some sort
of literary talent as a kid, like she enjoyed writing but she'd never gone to
college I don't even think she finished high school, so he encouraged her
to write poetry and since she had uh, an obsessive nature, she really took
to poetry. She started writing poetry when she was twenty-eight. And she
became really consumed with it she took, she was taking poetry classes
like adult education poetry classes at Boston University and she just kept

obsessively refining and editing her poetry using herself of course as her subject matter. Then I believe she received a scholarship to go to Breadloaf where she meets Robert Lowell. Anyway, so uh, she was raising her kid and writing like in the evenings obsessively and uh she started gaining attention getting things published slowly and uh then she realized when she did have all this success and she felt confident enough in herself, then she decided to fuck everything up. So she divorces Kato because she thought she should have more lovers, this was after Linda was in college, uh, so she divorces him, at this point she's won the Pulitzer Prize she's about to turn fifty I think she's teaching at, she's like full faculty at Boston University and her books are selling well so she decides to, ugh. So those things are going very well but she's very lonely because the men she, the men with whom she thought she was going to have these great love affairs never panned out. So she meets her good friend Maxine Kumin in the city in Boston to have lunch and sort of get her affairs in order and tell her where she wants her collection *The Awful Roaming toward God* to go. I guess if you're meeting a friend, I guess you could automatically come to the conclusion she's tying up loose ends, so she goes home, Anne Sexton goes home, she puts on her mother's fur, she goes into the garage, turns on the car, and uh, ugh, and kills herself. She was also a model. And she knew Sylvia Plath.

Marriage

Freud had a lot of good ideas even if now they seem old-fashioned, like that orgasms calm a woman down. And at the time he was working, Freud was working in Austria or Germany, Germany wasn't really a country yet then so it doesn't matter, at that time people maybe had totally forgotten that it used to be the conventional wisdom, um, it used to be normal to say, a regular saying that women always want sex and men just want to make them happy. Happy wife, happy life. In the Renaissance and even the Dark Ages, in those times people would say you could tell a newlywed by his skinny calves. Because his wife was working him out so hard with sex all the time. In those times people were coupling in all sorts of ways and if you listen to the murder ballads like "The Little Musgrave" then you know all the fuss about virginity, about women's purity, chastity belts and so on, was about old, not old but certainly middle-aged, say thirty-five- or forty-year-old men wanting to make sure they weren't tricked, weren't cuckolded by their teenage brides. There was coverture and women were property but most people were peasants and didn't own anything so when we think of bad marriage laws and sexism what we are thinking about is forty-year-old men marrying their friends' teenage daughters, so of course they were trying to keep the teenage boys away and of course the teenage girls were really in love with the teenage boys and of course the boys wanted to kill the fathers and take the girls, who were not their mothers but were somebody's mothers already at fifteen, sixteen, while the boys had to wait twenty more years to get married, if at all, because what if you're not the eldest son? How are you going to make money before jobs were invented, or if your family is too fancy for you to have a job and it would embarrass them? So we are really talking about the problems of a very few rich people and most everyone else was free to do what people usually do which is to pair off and sometimes stay in love forever and sometimes fight a lot but still stay together and sometimes split up and try again with someone else. But Freud came along and saw that the younger people want the old people out of the way, and not just for Marx's reasons although that makes it easier to understand cultures that respect their elders they usually have a different structure for getting and sharing money. But Freud saw that boys want to kill the dads and marry the moms and girls want to marry the dads but if they, if the boys make themselves into the dads by killing them, that tidies that one right up. Freud understood the teenage brain. He knew that we all want to pee on the fire to put it out.

Great Men of Science: Schumann

Uh, Schumann was studying to be a lawyer because that's what his parents wanted him to do or his mother rather, his father died. Instead he wanted to play the piano and be a famous pianist and he also took composition lessons with, Wieck was his name. Wieck. Anyway while he was studying with Wieck he was introduced to Wieck's daughter Clara you know Clara Schumann later and he fell in love with her and and he kept asking for her hand in marriage but her father kept refusing because Clara was a famous concert pianist at the time and didn't think Robert Schumann was good enough for her or something like that, I don't know. And so Robert Schumann wrote, I think that's when he wrote "Dichterliebe" because he was sad about Clara so "Dichterliebe" is all sad. In the meantime Schumann decides to make himself look better on paper so he gets his doctorate, which was pretty easy to do then, he just sent in some pieces and they gave him a doctorate. So he was a distinguished man you see. Still, Clara's father was not impressed. But finally when Clara turned eighteen they did get married and miraculously Wieck or begrudgingly Wieck gave them his consent. Not that it was needed anymore. I don't think. And Schumann was not a very successful composer but Clara was very successful as she was one of the most famous classical pianists or just pianists of the day. And Schumann wrote music critiques and was kind of angry all the time about other composers' work or their music composition because it wasn't good enough to see. He didn't think they were very good. Brahms. He liked Brahms. He gave Brahms a complex. So the story goes. And then uh, so Schumann starts hearing music in his head and turns out that

Schumann had syphilis a while back and it didn't get treated very well. He thought he took care of it but he didn't. So Schumann one day tries to uh he thinks he's hearing angels singing at him. And he liked it at first but I suppose that got a little wearing because then he threw himself in the Rhine. The Rhine's not that deep. Must have been cold though. Because it was the middle of winter. Anyway so because he did that Schumann was put in an insane asylum and it made Clara very sad as you can imagine. It sort of broke her. And it made Brahms nervous I guess and sad too. But um, while Schumann was there he wrote a little bit, not much, mostly just crazy people things because the syphilis had taken over, but he did write a violin concerto I think that was the last thing he wrote. Everyone thought he was crazy because it was too difficult and not many people, not many violinists played it after, not until Heifetz or some violinist started playing it regularly or at least brought it back out, blew the dust off of it. Anyway when Schumann died Clara was very upset. Don't think she wore black all the time but she might have. And Brahms was sad but I think Brahms was more in love with Clara. They spent a lot of time together but nothing ever happened. Maybe they touched hands one time on a bench and that fulfilled them sexually maybe.

Love

Of course it starts off like, there was an experiment once upon a time that
proves that we don't exist. I don't know! There are people who never stop
loving. Their beloved. Their love for their beloved keeps going
the same as it was, they light up the way they lit up the first time
they saw that person, that way forever. Their brain. Your brain is what's
lighting up but your eyes light up and your skin flushes and if you're a
woman maybe your joints lube up a little, I think that's what's really
happening when your knees go weak. Songs describe a lot of this
brain-body reaction. Sappho, maybe we could say Sappho is the first
songwriter, those were the first pop songs, with the jealousy and the melting
and the desperation like a good soul song, which all sound extra-desperate
because Berry Gordy made his singers, made them sing a
a third or something above what they thought was their range. Vocal range.
Which is also chemical if by chemical we can mean hormones, and it is also
a sneaky way to court ladies, to make yourself seem desperate or vulnerable.
Like a child. And also to stretch out of your range, which is physically
possible all the time but we don't have any reason like a mastodon
or a burning car. So pop music describes this brain-body reaction. But now
we know that there are brain chemicals that are, are spurting around
and flooding the brain and making it think, Okay, now I have to be ready
to run away or run toward or run with, run with this person. Away to a
cabin in the apple orchard. Back to paradise. Psychoanalysts say if you see
someone and you want to run away to a cabin in the apple orchard
with them you should run the other direction because it's just your

subconscious trying to get you into trouble so that you can give up, give up your ego? Maybe the subconscious is exactly right but it, the subconscious it hasn't gone through the Enlightenment or the Reformation or the Industrial Revolution or the Global Economy so when it says, That guy is like your dad when he was a young rake it's trying to help you out because that would have stood you in good stead for most of human history. But for some people they stop lighting up after a few years and it has yet to be studied I think whether the people who keep lighting up are in love with especially interesting people. If you fall in love with someone especially interesting your brain will keep making good love chemicals. If they are boring after a while you don't. Freud would make you a boring match. Mad hysterical crazy-making love is completely, um possible. Possible and reasonable and desirable. Maybe not a fairytale.

Self-esteem

You know how now we can look at the brain. We can see what the brain
is, is doing, where it's lighting up, not lighting up, I mean, the machines
attached to the brain are lighting up, but the brain is active. Like a muscle.
The brain is a muscle. It gets bigger if you work it out! If you tell children
that their brain gets bigger like a muscle if they do um, long division, or, or
if they try to read something hard like, like give them Lacan's mirror essay
or something where they will get it, something where they will get it if they
aren't, if they are made to just try, it's intuitive, you know? The baby
in the mirror, everyone gets that. The baby in the mirror. The baby
in the mirror is probably lighting up when it sees itself, its brain is lighting
up. This could be proof of self-love. Narcissus. No need for trophies—
self-esteem is innate. So the brain, which is getting bigger as it works
you can see it working out, or, well, you can see it's active, because the brain
is full of electricity, the body is full of electricity, not just the heart, lub-dub
lub-dub, in other countries the heart must speak something else, like those
weirdo French roosters, Coco-rico! Coco-rico! Which is, if you think
about it, a lot closer to what a rooster really sounds like, doodle? Doodle
is not a sound animals can make, that's advanced forward palate, I
think that's what the linguists call it, advanced stuff. And then th. Th is
even more advanced. That's why a lot of languages don't have it and just
have like, d instead. Dah. Duh. Maybe this is why the English, English
speakers thought, or think, still think, definitely still think that they're so
advanced. More advanced humans. With the fast food and rock 'n' roll and
democracy. It will always be the 1950s in the USA. Or maybe they

I mean, we, I'm incriminated too here, maybe we just light up more in the mirror. Maybe English-speaking people have more mirrors around them as, as babies. But Lacan is French. So: if you tell kids Try Harder instead of Good Job their brains will grow more and they will have better self-esteem.

Lucy

There's a story, at least one of the stories, about Lucy the chimp raised as
a human that's more about her sister and brother too. I heard this one from
at least two people, I think it's a, it's in a book. These scientists had other
children after they got Lucy and since Lucy was already in the house
in the home and was already being raised like a child, like they were
the younger children, were raised, they just always thought of her as
their big sister. It was normal, she was normal for them. Maybe
they realized something was a little different when they got older
but it could have taken a while or more likely it, it didn't matter by then.
Because they already loved her, like, thought of her as their sister. Not like
Nanny in *Peter Pan*, but have you seen that recently? Probably not, because
Disney doesn't make it anymore. It's racist. Really racist. "What Made the
Red Man Red?" Or worse really the way that the Indians are just playing
with the boys, I think the older brother, John, the one with the top hat
and umbrella and spectacles says They're sporting. Anyway they have that
St. Bernard who makes their beds and stacks their blocks and can basically
the film implies that she can read, or knows A-B-C anyway. But Lucy was
a real child in this family so the kids, I mean she and the other children
hung out together and played all the time. I guess they would anyway. And
one time they found a kitten in a vacant lot and Lucy killed it. Killed the
kitten. I don't know if it was like Lenny did the bunny in *Of Mice and Men* or
if it was on purpose, or more on purpose, because don't you think Lenny is
a little bit controlling? With the woman? Sad. Sad. But either way
the children were with her and they, I think at least the boy was maybe

a little scared that something was happening with Lucy, that she was going to become more like her chimp-self than her human-self, maybe she was going through puberty or almost there, when she went through puberty she got mad at her parents. Like you do. But anyway, he told. About the kitten. And the other sister, the youngest, she was very upset about this. Or maybe she told because she was young and didn't know how to lie to their parents and the brother was very upset about this. Either way they didn't talk for years. Because Lucy was sent away. But at the very end when she said goodbye to her sister she, Lucy gave the little sister a red poker chip which was a sign that she liked her or thought she was good or had positive feelings about her, at least. It was a way of communicating that the parents came up, devised when she was little because being a chimpanzee of course Lucy couldn't talk. But she could have learned sign so I don't know why they used chips. Maybe it was more scientific or faster for studies. Anyway that's what happened, how Lucy was sent away or why. Or that could have been some other chimp raised in a human family. Seems to happen a lot.

Great Men of Science: Thucydides

Okay so Alcibiades was a pupil of Socrates. He was also very beautiful
and uh, to many people Alcibiades and Socrates were opposites
where Alcibiades looked very beautiful and had a bad soul and Socrates
looked sort of, you know sort of ugly but had a good soul but that, uh
I don't know if Socrates had a good soul. So Alcibiades was a general
in the Peloponnesian War and before he went to war, the night before
he went to war he went out drinking with his friends and they were
they were sort of a wild bunch liked to party and have fun and, uh
the next morning Alcibiades was set to sail and he left Athens and, uh
that night a lot of, Hermes statues were sort of like the gnome statues
in France, those little gnomes, the Hermes statues, all their phalli were
cut off. From the Hermes statues. Anyway this made everyone in
Athens all crazy, like all the citizens in Athens crazy and somehow
everyone blamed Alcibiades for this uh, this uh, defacing if you will.
And uh, while he was on his way to, I think he was going to Sicily for
the failed, to help out with the failed Sicily expedition and, uh, he was
called back when he was almost to Sicily or he caught word that he was
wanted back in Athens because they wanted to put him on trial for
cutting off all the phalli of the Hermes statues and uh, and uh, this could
lead to uh, to uh, his death. Because he already was sort of unpopular
anyway and they were sort of, uh, Athens was sort of paranoid and starting
to lash out at all of its leaders. That's democracy for you. So when he heard
or uh, heard the news that he was being called back he suddenly jumped
ship I don't know if he literally did that but he escaped and ended up

defecting to Sparta. And while he was in Sparta he sort, he, he, he was very good at um, um, sort of a chameleon-like character, so whatever situation he found himself he could blend and become a part of that environment. And Spartans led a very different lifestyle a Spartan lifestyle if you will different from the Athenians but he got along very well until he slept with the Spartan king's daughter. Then the Spartan king, I think it was this I think, I think the Spartan king ordered him to be killed or something. Anyway so Alcibiades defected yet again but this time to Persia the old enemy or the continual enemy of Athens and Sparta and while he was in Sparta Alcibiades also gave like all the secrets of Athens, their military strategy, to the Spartans. So after that, now we're in Persia, so whilst in Persia Alcibiades becomes chummy with the Persian king and maybe he slept with the daughter of the Persian king maybe he didn't sleep with the daughter of the Spartan king, anyway he did some, I think he slept with the Persian king's daughter and the Persian king of course was not very happy about this and sent for the uh, the uh, for Alcibiades to be killed. I believe he escaped and made it back to Athens and they were excited that he was back. But they lost the war anyway because Persia decided in the end because they held all the power they had all the money, because Sparta and Athens were bankrupting themselves. Patience is a virtue.

War

The first war we know about, we know about the first war, recorded war
because there's a sculpture of it, a relief, the flat kind of sculpture that is
not that far off from a tablet really so it's like writing, it's recorded history.
It's a relief, a carving, of a bunch, a row, really, a row, or a rank? Is it a rank?
Like rank and file? Or a file? A file of soldiers in pointy helmets
with one big eye. Each. I mean they each have one big eye, not one big eye
for all of them. And they're carrying spears and the spears are carved in
such a way that you can't see who is holding them so it's not like here's a
row of soldiers with spears, it's like you get the sense that it's many many
many men with spears, many hands holding spears, and they're all moving
forward or in the same direction together as one. And there are a bunch of
feet sort of too and those are under the spears and like, it's like they're all
the heads with the eyes, like they're holding some enormous shield together
with holes for the spears to stick through but you can see the hands on
the spears so you know it's not a shield it's just, like, a rectangle that is either
representing the phalanx, the fist if you will, of the army. The army
as one fist. So there's that about war. The satisfaction of disciplining I think
they like to say, of disciplining the self, submitting to the will of the group.
And when the group is a whole country it can maybe be very satisfying
indeed to feel one's self submit to the group. So you fly a flag and support
the troops and that all feels really good and it also feels good to be one in
the group that marches and calls their senators and writes letters to the
paper about how the war is corrupt or poorly thought out or otherwise
a bad idea. And people protested early very early wars too, the women

protested the Peloponnesian War by not having sex with the men. They
weren't going to make more soldiers. But now we have machines, planes
well really they're like UFOs, we have drones to kill people. We don't have
to have a whole huge population of people just walk right into one another's
spears, really, they would just walk into each other's spears
Well, I'm in a war, I guess I have to charge and die. But now no one, or
not a lot of people in America anyway most people don't want to do that
because our sense of individuality is ultra-developed so we have to have
machines go and bomb very specific people like, individuals, because it
works both ways, individuality, so the leaders of our countries have kill
lists which is probably exactly like they did it 4000 years ago anyway, but
now we don't send a whole army to go get our enemies we just send a robot
plane. And sometimes it kills other people accidentally and we get upset if
they are children but really a lot lot lot less people die this way. It's utopic.
Like most wars. If we could just get everyone to live like us the world would
be perfect! And if we can't we get so mad, that was Achilles's problem, his
wrath. But that made him almost a god it was like he didn't care about this
life or this world didn't want to eat a peach just got mad when Agamemnon
took Briseis away from him not sad like he missed her or anything. And
he loved his friend. But it was his anger, anger that made Achilles godlike
and it still works that way, if you get super angry, righteously angry, you, it
makes you feel powerful and clean and perfect like a god.
That's why it's a sin, anger. Wrath. The worst one. Because it makes you
think you're a god and that you decide what's right. But that

is how we try to feel about war still because war the real kind of civilization war that we've had ever since we've had soldier as a specialization, that kind of war is what makes us human. Animals don't have wars. Except they do. Ants have wars, and they probably feel really really right when they're having a war too.

At rest, however, in the middle of everything, is the sun. For in this most beautiful temple, who would place this lamp in another or better position than that from which it can light up the whole thing at the same time?

—Nicolaus Copernicus, *De Revolutionibus*

Agriculture

But that was just the first war we know about. The difference would be that earlier, maybe there were battles and some tribes would go get other tribes' food or furs or clay pots or probably, unfortunately but probably women but then the tribe that was attacked and had their stuff stolen would regroup, they would regroup and go get their stuff and their women. But then once we started to have cities, food stored for years, agriculture, once we started to have large populations and civilizations then, that's when that's when you get like a whole civilization that has it out for another civilization and wants to ruin them. Run them off the earth. Because they think they're getting all the food or the women or the stuff or whatever. It's not even any more. Or it feels uneven, there's a fear of it not being fair, it's not fair that they get to have better stuff or more beautiful women or whatever and so the angry ones go to war. It's the caveman part of them we think, we say that that's our bad self but really the cavemen were probably a lot nicer. They didn't try to kill each others' whole cultures, at least as far as we know. They didn't make any art about it anyway.

Domestication

It's just like AIDS but only felines get it. It's like their version of AIDS.
But there has to be a different name for it. It's like, sickly. I cringe every
time I hear one of us say cat AIDS it's like ooh, really, are we still using
that term? Some people like calling it cat AIDS it's more dramatic. And
some cats, what is their belly from? The sagging? There are those cats that
don't have any fur. Those are freaky. The ones that have no tails, those are
pretty weird. I'm forgetting, from Darwin and evolution, if you have a
subdominant trait it will never increase, right? I don't remember any of
that stuff. I think it's that it will always go up but it will never increase
to the point of being dominant. So how do you breed scrappy bald cats?
How do you breed dog breeds like pugs where you have to inbreed them
and inbreed them so much that they end up with these horrible genetic
defects? Supposedly we are the result of thousands of years of selection
but why don't I feel that way about dogs? I can look at a husky and say
you are a beautiful dog. You are a gorgeous, gorgeous dog. Even a hound
dog. But some of these little scrappy things, abominations. What kind of
long arduous breeding process did somebody have to go through in some
barn somewhere to get you? But so many people love them. In cities
the way most of us live now, you don't want a greyhound, a lab, in your
apartment. You need a little lap dog. Teacup Chihuahua. Yeah, I couldn't
own a dog without two acres. Maybe, maybe, I could possibly settle for
what are most houses? Their backyards are like, a, an eighth of an acre?
If the dog wasn't that large, like, Shiba Inus? They kind of look like
foxes. Orange little dogs. They're very playful and fun. The other thing is

like, how much food dogs consume! But isn't dog food a new invention? Throughout years of history they were fed table scraps. I was talking to some people at the meat counter who were buying steaks for their dogs. Of course it can't be Grade D ground chuck. They buy them fucking sirloin. And this guy was sort of laughing at himself, he was like, Do you believe what I'm doing? Do you know how much money I spend every day on this dog? If I were doing that I would expect my dog to eat with its paws at the table. Linen napkin. I imagine those dogs are pretty well-trained. My pet peeve with these, with pets, is that dogs aren't trained anymore. They can roll over and shake hands but they can't obey when it really matters. I see these little ladies at the park like, Come here! Come! And their dog is just running and they're saying, It's okay! He's a sweet dog! But no one says, Stay away my dog is a bastard. I like, one thing I like is that I don't expect any decisions out of my cat, she's not trying to force her views or politics on me like a dog would. We just know that nothing is going to transgress the space between us. But that's people who like cats anyway. People who like dogs would be like, Cats are assholes. I guess I have a hard time with entities that are completely dependent. I don't like it. It weirds me out. Unlike all other animals, dogs seem to actually want to make humans happy. We train them to be these soft, we are given all these dogs, hunting dogs that are like, badass and we turn them into these I need your pets! I need you to pet me! These pet-needing machines. Whereas a cat, you know, you can forget it's there. It can forget you're there. I've been trying to move very slowly so that mine won't even notice.

Lucy, Part Two

The monkey. The chimp. There was this couple. I think they were scientists. And they decided that they wanted to raise a chimpanzee. Idiots. And so they went to a circus to acquire said chimpanzee. And they named her Lucy. And they decided that they were going to raise Lucy just like they would raise their daughter. They would treat Lucy exactly the same. She would sleep with them, not that, I guess you wouldn't sleep with your parents. They would watch television together. They would read to her. And chimpanzees are fine until they reach adolescence. 'Cause then they go crazy because they want the sex. And hormones. And, and, and, um so trouble well, trouble started happening when Lucy entered adolescence and their experiment had to, their experiment had to, they had to curtail their experiment because she would be very violent and um, and was very confrontational. So naturally they built a cage in their house where Lucy would live. And when Lucy, as most people when they enter adolescence become interested in sex. And the interesting thing is that Lucy because she was raised exclusively with humans and was not around chimpanzees, other chimpanzees, was attracted to humans. So in keeping with their experiment these people decided to buy a, uh, a *Playgirl* for Lucy and Lucy masturbated to the *Playgirl*. Um, oh there's more to the story. So then they're at a crossroads these two scientists because they don't know what to do with Lucy. So 'cause they can't let her, they can't, they looked into all of these natural habitats that she could live in or you know, zoos, but all the places that they you know, visited, made them very depressed because they had to, you know they loved Lucy like their daughter. Though what parents would watch their daughter masturbate, you know I'm just saying. Or lock them in a cage. So in the meantime they hired someone to come and help, help them take care of Lucy. And the person who came in was someone in their twenties early twenties who was also a biologist or um, I don't know. And she came in to help out Lucy and this woman or this young woman actually got along really well because Lucy viewed her as a peer. She was sort of rebelling against her parents but viewed this young woman as a peer and so they got along pretty well. So in the end the mother and father decided that they would ship Lucy to this island where other chimps live, in, somewhere off of South America does that make any sense? Do chimps live there? That's wrong it was, was Africa. Somewhere off of South Africa. Or is Ghana in Africa? It was Ghana. An island off of Ghana. Are there islands off of Ghana? Is Ghana on the coast? So. An island off of Ghana. So they decided they were going to have this young woman, and, go with Lucy to Ghana and introduce, sort of wean Lucy off of her, off of humans and introduce her to other chimps. This took years. This woman was there for years. And it started off, out where, 'cause Lucy was so interested in human things she didn't care about chimp things. So Lucy wanted to eat this young woman's food, would only eat her food would only stay with her wouldn't go away and was just connected with her the whole time. And Lucy had, her favorite toy was a mirror and so the young woman realized that this wasn't working very well and that she had to literally separate herself somehow from Lucy but at the same time remain, have some

contact with her. So she ended up contacting the military in Ghana and
somehow convinced them to make a giant cage for her. And they shipped
the cage over, flew the cage over and the young woman put all of her stuff in
the cage and locked herself in the cage so that Lucy couldn't get to her. And
there was no roof in the beginning so Lucy would sleep on top of
the cage, would pee on her, would do the other thing on her too and it
would rain and she was exposed to the climate, whatever. And the more
upsetting thing was that Lucy stopped eating, wouldn't, because she would
only eat people food so she wasn't hunting she wasn't looking for food
which the young woman tried to show her how to do. Like, the
young woman before this would go to the forest with her and eat berries
or eat things showing her how to get off, food off of trees and, but Lucy
wouldn't have any of it. So Lucy's starving to death and um, sort of laying
next to the cage. But one day something happens where she finally goes
and gets food for herself. And begins to, to, you know participate
with the other chimps, starts feeding herself. So at this point the
young woman decides that it's time for her to leave. This had been
three years, like, this whole process. I hope she got paid well! Probably not.
So she leaves and she decides, she leaves and she decides that she will
come back in two years to the island to see Lucy. Which she does. And she
brings with her some of Lucy's favorite things like her mirror and some of
her other toys. She goes back to the island and Lucy comes out of the, uh
the forest with the other chimps and um, approaches the woman and
the, I guess the older woman now, I mean, she's not old. Approaches

the woman and essentially gives her a hug like wraps her arms around her and holds her very tight and then runs away with the other monkeys. But when she's on the island like, staying on the island, the woman, Lucy follows her or you know, will come and see her or, and, and, um, the, the woman said that that it felt like symbolic when Lucy hugged her she felt as though, of course she's just reading into this but you know, maybe the woman felt as though Lucy were acknowledging her but was going to the other chimps as though I'm choosing this, I'm choosing the other chimps. So the woman leaves and she decides to come back two years later. She comes back two years later and this time Lucy doesn't, she can't find Lucy, Lucy doesn't approach them on the island at all and she discovers uh, the skeletal remains of a chimp in the cage that she locked herself in, in the cage, and she says it's Lucy because it has the same gap in its front teeth that Lucy had and was the same height and there was something else that made it seem like Lucy and um, she thinks what happened because Lucy was missing her hands was that poachers got her and that she was an easy target because she was very comfortable with humans so if poachers approached she would be the first to approach them so she probably was killed. But I don't know why she was in the cage. It's a mystery.

Evolution

Like how whales came from camels. Yes, whales are camels who just
they just kept going farther and farther and farther out into the sea for, um
the vegetation, the sea, the seaweed, maybe sea grapes, I don't know
it would have been the, um, the Indian Ocean. What grows there?
The camels were living in India. Or maybe Africa. Is Africa on the Indian
Ocean? Yes. Of course. Somali pirates. And the Sahara. So they
the camels were living in Africa and they had to go to the ocean to get
something to eat. And they just, the camels just got better and better
at swimming, like their hooves, their hooves got wider and softer like
paddles and their, their nostrils moved up higher and higher and they just
kept going farther out for the seaweed and then maybe they didn't really
need teeth as much and their teeth turned into, um, what is it, baleen?
Baleen. Yes. So the best camels started, um, developed these features, and
they, they, they um, it's not like they killed the other camels but the camels
with these good sea features, characteristics that were good for the sea
they survived. They lived and they ate more of the seaweed and had more
babies and passed on their paddles and noses and everything. And then
they just never came back to land. They became whales. They came out
of the ocean, they lived on land for millions of years, and they went back
to the ocean. Later everybody! They lived in the Sahara. That's basically
the best story about evolution. It took millions and millions of years, but
camels became whales. That's the power of evolution. Whales are actually
camels. I mean, why do you think they breathe air?

Sharks

So I'm taking this taxidermy class and it starts and we have to have bodies
I mean, I think we have to bring a dead thing to class, to taxidermy, maybe
not the first day, not the first day but the next week the second class I mean
I thought that would be on the materials, or required on the syllabus but
it's in the course fee. It's built in. They're giving us the dead things I mean
we we already paid for them when we signed up, signed up for the class.
Registered. So it's birds. We're doing birds. Which seems like it would be
neater. Birds seem less messy I mean they seem like they would shrivel up
when they die, like just dry up just dessicate or something. Dry right up
into a neat little corpse. And then we cut the skin off and put it back on.
More like a reptile like, like making a crocodile bag or um, a crocodile pelt
if you will well, I know you wouldn't call it a pelt because pelts are hair but
you know what I mean just a little piece of reptile skin. Bird skin I mean.
But birds are warm-blooded. I know they aren't reptiles but I don't know
I don't know how they have warm blood but they aren't mammals.
Warm blood and a two-chamber heart. I remember that they have a
two-chambered heart. In, out, in, out, good, bad, love, hate. That's why
birds are so crazy about people. A parrot thinks, he thinks, thinks the
woman, his owner, the woman who owns him is his life's mate. Soul mate.
Parrot and lady. Stevie Nicks. *Bella Donna!* But anyway, birds. Birds have
warm blood, and bones, like mammals, not cartilage. Fish have cartilage.
Birds have bones like mammals, not cartilaginous skeletons as fish do.
But actually fish have bones I know that fish have bones so it's sharks

I'm thinking of, sharks don't have bones and yes! I remember now. Sharks are not fish. They are just sharks. I think I remember this. Sharks are their own thing. Shark.

Toxoplasmosis

Cats are very dangerous because apparently they have or they can have a parasite. And this parasite somehow, it gets in a position where it can move to somewhere in the cat's brain and tell, sort of dictate what it should do. And. No. That was wrong. There's a parasite that lives in the feces of the cat. And this parasite is very adaptive it, oh, this is terrible, it basically the argument is that this parasite lives in the feces of cats and when cat people, because the cat has this parasite and they clean the litter box is that this parasite can enter the body the human body and because a parasite's main goal is to survive within the human body and live off the human body. There's an ant, no, a plant that does this to ants. Makes them impale themselves on the plant. Or a parasite makes them impale themselves, I think it's working with, teamed with, what is that, symbiosis? Working with the plant. But with cat people, um, the parasite needs cats to spread its larvae so it goes to a person's brain and makes them like cats. Makes people crazy about cats.

Transubstantiation

I don't even know what the hell that is.

Great Men of Science: Tycho Brahe

You know how some people are famous but we don't know why? Or because they're friends with someone, with someone important or because they have some funny quirk or affectation or something? Once I was in a coffee roaster, roastery café, a coffeehouse in San Francisco, and everyone there had a, a funny affectation or really just a prop or something. There was a man with a parrot! He had to be at least forty-two years old. And the guy behind the counter, the barista, but not really, he was just selling the coffee not making it, that guy made fun of me a little because I didn't recognize the Led Zeppelin on the stereo. They had records. Vinyls. Which are cumbersome and expensive so they are kind of like props. But they're coming back because people want, people like to, when people buy something they like to get a thing. An object. Nobody's very excited about buying collections of ones and zeros. Except in app form. Playing games on your phone. So Tycho Brahe had a mother of a, a whopper of a prop, he had a gold nose because his first nose, his original nose was cut off, was nicked, shaved off in a duel. I used to think it fell off because of syphilis. Syphilis really got to people before antibiotics were invented. Everyone had it. It rots you. Parts of you get gangrene and if it happens in your brain you go crazy and die and they used to try to cure it with mercury. Isak Dinesen had it or anyway Karen Blixen, her alter ego her *Out of Africa* character had it, but in her case it was a blessing sort of she couldn't have done all of the things she did in Africa with children or at least it would have been harder and well, the big thing is that probably Denys the pilot, the big game hunter, he wouldn't have happened if she had a bunch of kids but then Anna Karenina had a child and that didn't stop Vronsky though they are two totally really different guys. Denys is more like a Levin. Or Keats. Keats died of, of consumption, TB, the very Romantic tuberculosis but probably he wouldn't have even, even gotten it if he didn't poison himself, wasn't already poisoning himself with mercury and that was, probably was because he had syphilis. He went to Oxford. There were a lot of, of prostitutes there at that time there were something like ten percent of the population or maybe just the women the female population in London was prostitutes. There were a lot of young men of course. In Oxford. I don't know where Tycho Brahe fits into that although he is also hanging out with royalty like most everyone in history in the history that we know about of course, he's in the court and he's a scientist. With a pet moose and a golden nose and he liked wine women and song. The Falstaff of scientists! Which is why he got backstabbed um, double-, double-crossed by Johannes Kepler. Kepler was his assistant. The thing that we think of as Kepler's invention or theory, Kepler's Law or the idea that you can see a point in the sky a star or a planet and that you can then plot it for many days in a row and that this somehow, this proves that the earth and other planets move on an orbit, on orbits around the sun it's similar in some ways to Galileo later, not much later actually, proving that the earth is not the center of the universe, the solar system or this solar system at least, anyway, that idea in another form was discovered earlier by Tycho Brahe. Ptolemy thought of it and Tycho Brahe tried to prove it with the, the better optics of the time and his record-keeping but

they both sort of stopped, they stopped short of figuring out what
the actual orbits would look like and how to solve, resolve the problem of
planets going in loops, having loopy orbits. But Kepler stole Brahe's ideas
or really probably he just kept at his work after he died, he was kind of
honoring him that way and he was in correspondence with Galileo but
Kepler actually drew out, actually diagrammed the orbits that Ptolemy and
Tycho Brahe calculated but excused with magic or with religion, that is the
idea of the Fifth Element, that planets are made of ectoplasm or something
not ectoplasm that's ghosts but something unearthly. Fog or holograms.
Kepler though, he, he thought that God must be rational, God, if God
is omniscient and omnibenevolent I guess then God would be a
friendly rational God and would not make a universe we can't understand.
God doesn't trick us. For Kepler. Ptolemy probably had good, very good
reasons for thinking maybe God is pretty tricky. But anyway now Tycho
is only known for his fun-loving silly affectations and that he died because
he didn't go to the bathroom, he held it all through a fancy dinner with
the King, one of those dinners where they serve live peacock or whatever
crazy horrible stuff they did when they were transitioning from the
Dark Ages to the Enlightenment. And for maybe being murdered by Kepler
he is known for that too and everyone thought it was mercury poisoning so
he was exhumed, his body was dug up, actually that man has been dug up
at least twice that we know of, poor dead Tycho Brahe, no grave can hold
his body down. But there wasn't enough mercury in his mustache or his
teeth so it probably was a bladder infection from being too polite to excuse

himself or just enjoying the beef and whisky too much though I think that's gout, right? Also his nose was brass not gold they found that, they tested his nose too just like, I guess, while they were in there or while they had him out or, you know, While we're at it. So don't hold it. It's not good for you. And Keats was a real young man not a poet-ghost-angel.

Missionaries

We did this for church. We let go all these balloons, well, one balloon
each. With Bible verses on the cards I think about friendship or loving one
another, you know children are always taught first, at least I was taught first
that verse John 3:16. God loves the world that means God loves you
and you love your neighbor. Keep your hands to yourself. But I think
putting that on a, on a balloon, it was supposed to be an introduction to
evangelism. Or for a big ending to Vacation Bible School week. I think one
kid, I think her balloon went to China. Maybe the Philippines. I had a
beautiful plaid Thermos, the classic plaid, for my milk I think, and
my teacher dropped it. It was glass. She was probably fifteen. I also had
a peanut butter and jam sandwich and Doritos. We were outside in a row
on an asphalt curb we were watching uh, an eclipse of the sun.
Very carefully through a pinhole. I was so, so scared I would burn my eyes if
I made one wrong move! And then at the end of the week we let
our balloons go and I probably looked right at the sun when we were
watching them float up anyway. Although that might have been
a different year.

Memory

Like in the movie *Memento*. I think it's related to light. Light also has like
something to do with short-term memory where if you're in constant light
you lose your short-term memory. That's what happened to my friend who
went to Antarctica. You can only stay in Antarctica six months or you go
crazy. Because there's too much light. Once I was in a kitchen and we were
making Thanksgiving and they had a very strange light that kept flickering
and every time it happened it seemed to erase my memory of what had
just happened. Suddenly I felt the importance of light in memory. I felt
the connection very strongly. David Lynch. And David Byrne, David Byrne
and the sparkly lights and high sparkly notes because people take cocaine
at the disco.

Great Men of Science: Proust

Proust was a socialite in his early life and like maybe a drunk too because you know that goes hand in hand with being a socialite or at least a good one. So I think he realized one day, I think when he was in his late thirties, that he had wasted so much of his life that he went to his room or maybe it was his attic and he lined it with cork and he slept during the day and wrote at night and then he wrote the seven volumes. And, uh, they're all about him piecing together his drunken memories of the past.

Moon Landing

NASA has no idea how to get back to the moon. When they were doing all their formulas and building all their ships it was all done with slide rules and that, they had, they, they had, there were so many people working on it and so many different minds and they had no computers so none of it was retained. It was all written down on scraps of paper and then it was all immediately built and then once they built it they lost all the paperwork. They just lost, they have no paperwork. They don't have it. That's absolutely fascinating. That at one point we had the knowledge and we made the knowledge but we didn't take precautions to keep it. But other people think that it was a hoax.

The Sublime

Sublimity is Kant, er, from Kant, though I imagine the idea of it existed before. I guess the general gist is the feeling of being on a cliff, this is a very simplified version, being on a cliff looking over the cliff at the smallness or the expanse, the, the uh, expanse the, the expansiveness of what's below the cliff or beyond the horizon and the feeling, sublimity is the feeling of the initial terror and awe, feeling of both terror and awe. That's it.

Great Men of Science: St. Paul

So Saul, who is who Paul was before he was St. Paul, before he was on the Road to Damascus and saw God or saw, saw a bright light like heat lightning or maybe some kind of weird eclipse or seizure of some kind or something, Saul-Paul is chasing Christians around the Roman Empire really hunting them, not like a gladiator, more like, like the bad sheriff terrorizing the Christians, the opposite of Billy the Kid, no flash, no grin no, no, beautiful Spanish ladies in love with him, well, maybe some, he was all over the Mediterranean but probably the Spanish ladies or really the ladies who would be Spanish, the pre-Spanish ladies, didn't love him at all anyway. So Saul is riding his horse through the desert to Damascus and like Billy the Kid the sun hits him so hard in the face, right in the face like a giant golden fist, but soft, but firm, like a father, kind of like it hit Hölderlin who was all about the union of opposites. Which God loves of course. If you were supposed to be everywhere and be in everything then you would have to love the union of opposites, right? And Celan is kind of happy about Hölderlin or at least he doesn't think it's tragic only, like Heidegger seems to. Pallaksch, pallaksch. So God knocks Saul right off his horse and then in some paintings and sculptures Saul is writhing on the ground like he's trying to get away from God or the light or whatever you want to call it and maybe he's also in pain or abject terror. And then in some depictions he's lying there open to whatever is going to happen like he's in a meditative state or something. We don't know. We weren't there. But God tells Saul he's been doing it wrong all this time and he has to make a complete one-eighty and become a Christian and start helping the Christians instead of hunting them and so Paul says, Yes, whatever you say God. And he starts to bring his bad sheriff attitude to Christianity and he rounds them all up and makes them start having some standards so they don't seem like such a crazy cult because Paul knows what the Roman officials want to see in a religion and it's some uniformity because, after all, they were pretty much fascists. So Paul writes a bunch of letters to all these different Roman outposts and he tells the Christians how to act so that they seem legitimate and more like a real church than just a bunch of weird semi-Dionysian cannibal cults, which was not helping them at all. He becomes a subversive sort of, but a kind of conservative subversive, union of opposites, subverting the Roman Empire and the Jewish leaders but also conservative about women wearing headcoverings and not speaking and everyone giving ten percent of their money, giving tithes to start the church so it had some infrastructure. And he becomes a saint because he helps, he helps the Christians unify by having standards and making them a little more in line with old-fashioned Judaism but unfortunately most of those standards are not so good for women or for gays or really for anyone that the Roman Empire or the orthodox Jews wouldn't recognize as a leader. But he was doing the best he could. He made a promise to God because he was struck by the sun. God smited, God smote him, not with, like plagues or locusts or leprosy but he smited him with the sun.

The Afterlife

I think this was. The 19th century. It was a man who was obsessed with figuring out if there were any actual afterlife and this woman who was a psychic, a purported psychic. A medium. For the other world. And he went to visit her and they were trying to come up with an experiment to prove without a doubt that the afterlife existed. So they decided because she could commune with the, with the dead that he would kill himself and she would wait a day and when he got, got to the afterlife he was supposed to tell her that there was an afterlife. Talk to her. From the dead. So the man went home and killed himself. And she waited. But he never contacted her. He never told her.

Exoplanets

There are other worlds they have not told you of, I wish to speak to you.
Sun Ra is alive and well on some far away planet with Elvis. They're
orbiting like Xanadu or some shit. Because music and art often um, um
understand the way the brain works before the neuroscience catches up
like, so Proust and the madeleine knew about how memory works with
tastes and smells like how a smell can take you right back and it feels really
really real, really, really, real, really is just a lot of real. So it can, the smell
the taste of the sponge cake can take you back to the memory of that taste
or smell immediately. It's like having a shortcut on your computer to a
certain file or something although the brain works nothing like a computer
which is the trouble with, with this idea that if we can just make a program
that contains all of your memories all your idiosyncrasies all your special
personality then you will live forever through that program, it will be like
you never died. Although I don't know where the programs would be stored
or how they will run or how they will continue to make new experiences
so that you feel like you're still living and it's not just, like, a super-awesome
autobiography, like a virtual auto-, or I mean, like *Being John Malkovich*.
And before that *The Autobiography of Alice B. Toklas*. Gertrude Stein
knew all about the brain. But since you can't freeze yourself and the
Fountain of Youth isn't real and, I guess that's why we're so into vampires
because we never want to die. Jim Gustafson said, "Driving back the edge
with art that cares," and Paul Celan was all about the abyss, approaching
the abyss, getting right, right up to the lip of it, whether it's death or, or
the sun burning out or forgetting your childhood or being inside a

computer forever, all ones and zeros, all of this stuff is about not dying. Because the problem of philosophy which is really the problem of consciousness is, Why do I have to have a body? And how do I get out of here? We want to experience the body because the body is how we have a consciousness (madeleines, memory) but it is also how we die because the consciousness could go on forever (computers, poetry) but the body can't. Unless you're a vampire. Or a zombie. Is it better to eat brains than to be dead-dead? Is that the question we're asking ourselves with zombies? People say it's about immigration and difference but I think it's just about our fear of the dead. It's pretty basic. So because we're so afraid of death we're looking for other worlds outside our solar system which just means, means planets of other suns and maybe one of them probably, it's more likely than not, it's likely there is another planet with advanced life on it or at least life. I don't know how to judge advanced or not. We like to, or at least we usually think of extraterrestrial life, I mean outside of the movies, as amoebas and things other primordial soup-type things. Because it's too freaky to have other people, other beings we would recognize as our equivalent, humanoid or whatever, out there. We would want to have sex with them and kill them. So that we go on forever.

Lorem Ipsum

Neither is there anyone who loves, pursues, or desires pain itself because it is pain. But occasionally circumstances occur in which toil and pain can procure some great pleasure. To take a trivial example: who undertakes laborious physical exercise, except to obtain some advantage from it? Who has any right to find fault with someone who chooses to enjoy a pleasure that has no annoying consequences? Or one who avoids pain that produces no resultant pleasure? Yet we denounce with righteous indignation and dislike people who are so beguiled and demoralized by the charms of pleasure in the moment, so blinded by desire, that they cannot foresee the pain and trouble that are bound to ensue—when equal blame belongs to those who fail to uphold their duties because they are weak-willed, which is the same as saying they shrink from toil and pain.

Moon Landing, Part Two

So that was pretty much Stanley Kubrick. I'm done. That's it!

Actroids

I was watching this movie about images and it's mostly in Asia. Special dances, flowers, dances that make the dancers look like flowers or at least their hands. And at one point there's a beautiful young woman gazing into the camera and then her mouth drops open a little bit and by the way her mouth, her jaw moves, you can tell she's been turned off. You can tell she's a robot. You can't tell while she's making eye contact with you but she moves and there's a, something wrong with it. It's not quite right. Probably because you can tell that it's slower or something that, it's not like you can really tell this from looking but instead of an electrical impulse being sent from her brain to her mouth it's, well, it's still an electrical impulse being sent from the programmer's or the inventor's instructions which are really just a basic grid—body parts on the top, on the X axis and kinds of movements on the Y axis, something like that—but it still takes longer than it does for natural, human electricity to communicate commands. To our body. So we can tell and it's creepy. Uncanny. Occult. Dr. Frankenstein. But now that we know more about the brain we also know that we aren't really in control of the impulses that tell our mouth to move, either. So we are the robots of ourselves. Though that begs the question of what our selves are. And who is in charge of them. And free will. There was also a man in the movie who put a bag on his head and covered it in mud and made himself into a doll. A manikin. He put matches on his eyes, in the mud where the eyes would be.

Auto-Tune

Every singer uses it. Every singer uses it now, except for Neko Case. Except for Neko Case and Nelly Furtado. Remember Nelly Furtado? Everyone else uses Auto-Tune because if they don't they'll sound like indie rock, not pop singers. Who now sound like rappers. Because of Auto-Tune. Auto-Tune works by taking out the half-tones. By taking out the half-tones you make humans sound like synthesizers. You can't hear the shift between notes. Auto-Tune takes a note and pulls it apart in time. Then Auto-Tune looks for moments. Moments when the singer is not singing the main note. Moments when their voice wavers, perhaps. Moments of imperfection. If perfection is the note. And Auto-Tune takes those moments out. Auto-Tune very carefully slides out those moments of imperfection. No. Auto-Tune doesn't care. It doesn't have to be careful in order to do things right. Auto-Tune pulls out the imperfections and then pushes the sound back together as though imperfections were never there. As though the human voice could move from one note to the next with no transition, like a synthesizer. As though the human voice could hold one note forever without moments of imperfection. Milliseconds of undetectable imperfection. And we can't, we humans. Humans can't hear the difference unless the song wants us to. Cher wanted us to. T-Pain wanted us to. Britney Spears wanted us to. Britney Spears is always trying to prove to us that she is not a robot.

Great Men of Science: Koko

Feet is her word for men and lip is her word for woman. Remember the book, *Koko and Her Kitten?* All Ball. That was the kitten's name. Maybe because he didn't have a tail. He was all ball. So when she was captured as a baby her story of it, about that, is, Feet come feet feet no mother mother mother mother. So sad. She has a lot of words and makes things up, too. If someone makes her mad she calls them Toilet Devil. Also she had a boyfriend. I think his name was Mike but Mike didn't take to signing, to language very well. He just liked to say Meat. Or he wouldn't have been saying it, you know what I mean. When they, the researchers who live with them, with the gorillas, I think they live in a house, too, like people, when they asked him to use it in a sentence he signed, Meat meat meat meat meat. Which you can actually do with, oh, what is the word? With buffalo. Buffalo buffalo buffalo Buffalo buffalo. As in buffalo the animals from Buffalo, New York, fool other buffalos from Buffalo. I don't know why you would ever write that except to do it. But I don't think there are any other words that work that way so that's probably a good enough reason! So the hope was that Koko and Mike would have a baby but I don't know if they ever did or if they did it took a long time. She didn't like him much because he was a dunce. She liked people and All Ball. But All Ball got hit by a car. Koko cried and then she signed, Sleep, cat.

Dance

Oh, the little bird with the pink paper clip! Have you ever seen pictures of a, a bower? A bower bird's bower? It's not a nest it's more like an arbor but they make, they make it and everyone's is different, they make it out of little bits and bobs and things they find lying around like any other bird makes a nest. But they have, each bower bird has, and these are only the males by the way, the male birds make the bower, they have different styles. Aesthetics. So one will be really into one particular nut, the shape of this smooth round brown kind of shiny nut, and will just make a sort of carpet of these nuts leading up to a tucked-away little mating spot. Revolving bed, remote control hi-fi. So the minimalist nut guy will be next door to some, well, I don't know how much territory they need maybe not next door but there will be other bower birds who are making bowers with everything blue they can find or all the candy wrappers and foil potato chip bags and pop tabs around or with a certain leaf or flower bud. They like pattern and repetition. Like us. Three black medicine balls next to three black stockpots. So the ladybird stops by after the bower is all built and decorated and she she checks it out and the male does a little dance of some kind or sings a song. And she decides. One of the little birds in *National Geographic* had a pink paper clip to fling into the air at the end the end of his dance. She didn't like it. The first one, anyway. So he had to go find the paper clip in the bushes after, afterward and get ready for the next one to drop by. He wasn't, he was undaunted. Someone is going to like it. But this dance they do it's, it's, is not really real dance. Dance scientifically if it's dance, needs to be to a beat. Moving to an external beat.

And changing with the tempo. And it turns out that very few animals, very few species can do this. Scientists watched a bunch of YouTube videos of animals dancing and they, they figured out which ones were just mimicking a trainer's movements and which ones were spontaneously moving and they studied them. And actually it turns out that only humans and parrots and Asian, Indian elephants can dance. Especially this parrot Snowball who was left behind when his owner went to college. So her parents took Snowball to the bird shelter and showed the bird people that he could dance to the Backstreet Boys. Not very well. But it was dancing. And that led to the study that found out about parrots, elephants, and people. All of whom can speak or mimic, at least approximate speech. So actually, as it, it turns out maybe dancing and singing are linked. And when we watch the Backstreet Boys or Michael Jackson that's why we're so happy, they're doing dancing and singing at the same time and that's something that is really really human and also maybe a reenactment of ritual, I don't know why I think that, but maybe because of rain dances and the other mythic, mating dances, what we think of when we think about early dance. The Grecian urn, more happy, happy love. Or how the *Footloose* kids, John Lithgow, got the no dancing law overturned with the Bible. The verse. They danced.

ACKNOWLEDGMENTS

This book was inspired by conversations with Tucker Fuller, and first encouraged by *Tin House,* and by Simon Marriott of The Society for Curious Thought.

Paul Beisner, Jeffrey Schultz, Jennifer Metsker, Raymond McDaniel, Ann Marie Thornburg, Rebecca Porte, Kodi Scheer, and Forrest Gander were extraordinarily generous and thoughtful in their advice on the manuscript at various stages. I am lucky to be part of an inspiring community of writers and artists; it was especially helpful to talk about these poems with Julie Babcock, Joseph Chapman, David Ward, Robyn Anspach, Catherine Calabro, Alana DeRiggi, Onna Solomon, John Ganiard, Russell Brakefield, and Gina Balibrera. Stephanie Soileau, Elizabeth Wetmore, Van Jordan, Michael Byers, Eileen Pollack, and Stephanie Cabot also gave invaluable support.

"Fur" and "Fashion" are for my dad.

"Great Men of Science: Anne Sexton" is for Gillian White.

"Marriage" is for Karen McConnell and Nate Mills.

"Lucy" is for my mom.

"War" is for Doug Trevor.

"Domestication" is for my brother and sister-in-law.

"Sharks" is for Katie Jaeger.

"Exoplanets" is for Ken Mikolowski.

"Auto-Tune" is for Jeff Schultz.

"Great Men of Science: Koko" is for Dana Kletter.

"Dance" is for Steph Soileau.

ABOUT THE AUTHOR

Megan Levad's poems have appeared in *Tin House, Fence, Denver Quarterly, Mantis,* the Everyman's Library anthology *Killer Verse,* and London art and fashion magazine *AnOther.* She also writes lyrics for composers Tucker Fuller and Kristin Kuster. A native of rural Iowa, Megan lives in Ann Arbor, where she is the Assistant Director of the Helen Zell Writers' Program at the University of Michigan.

TAVERN BOOKS

Tavern Books is a not-for-profit poetry publisher that exists to print, promote, and preserve works of literary vision, to foster a climate of cultural preservation, and to disseminate books in a way that benefits the reading public.

We publish books in translation from the world's finest poets, new works by innovative writers, and revive out-of-print classics. We keep our titles in print, honoring the cultural contract between publisher and author, as well as between publisher and public. Our catalog, known as The Living Library, sustains the visions of our authors, ensuring their voices are alive in the social and artistic discourse of our modern era.

ABOUT THE WROLSTAD
CONTEMPORARY POETRY SERIES

To honor the life and work of Greta Wrolstad (1981-2005), author of *Night is Simply a Shadow* (2013) and *Notes on Sea & Shore* (2010), Tavern Books invites submissions of new poetry collections through the Wrolstad Contemporary Poetry Series during an annual reading period.

This series exists to champion exceptional literary works from young women poets through a book publication in The Living Library, the Tavern Books catalog of innovative poets ranging from first-time authors and neglected masters to Pulitzer Prize winners and Nobel Laureates. The Wrolstad Contemporary Poetry Series is open to any woman aged 40 years or younger who is a US citizen, regardless of publication history.

For more information visit: tavernbooks.com/wrolstad-series

THE LIVING LIBRARY

Arthur's Talk with the Eagle by Anonymous,
translated from the Welsh by Gwyneth Lewis

Ashulia by Zubair Ahmed

Buson: Haiku by Yosa Buson,
translated from the Japanese by Franz Wright

*Poems 1904 by C. P. Cavafy,
translated from the Greek by Paul Merchant

Who Whispered Near Me by Killarney Clary

The End of Space by Albert Goldbarth

Six-Minute Poems: The Last Poems
by George Hitchcock

The Wounded Alphabet: Collected Poems
by George Hitchcock

Hitchcock on Trial
by George Hitchcock

*The Boy Changed into a Stag Clamors
at the Gate of Secrets* by Ferenc Juhász,
translated from the Hungarian by David Wevill

My Blue Piano by Else Lasker-Schüler,
translated from the German by Eavan Boland

Archeology by Adrian C. Louis

Fire Water World & Among the Dog Eaters
by Adrian C. Louis

Ocean by Joseph Millar

Under an Arkansas Sky by Jo McDougall

*What the Dead Have Always Known by Jo McDougall

Petra by Amjad Nasser,
translated from the Arabic by Fady Joudah

The Fire's Journey: Part I by Eunice Odio,
translated from the Spanish by Keith Ekiss
with Sonia P. Ticas and Mauricio Espinoza

*The Fire's Journey: Part II by Eunice Odio,
translated from the Spanish by Keith Ekiss
with Sonia P. Ticas and Mauricio Espinoza

*The Fire's Journey: Part III by Eunice Odio,
translated from the Spanish by Keith Ekiss
with Sonia P. Ticas and Mauricio Espinoza

*The Fire's Journey: Part IV by Eunice Odio,
translated from the Spanish by Keith Ekiss
with Sonia P. Ticas and Mauricio Espinoza

Duino Elegies by Rainer Maria Rilke,
translated from the German by Gary Miranda

Twelve Poems about Cavafy by Yannis Ritsos,
translated from the Greek by Paul Merchant

Glowing Enigmas by Nelly Sachs,
translated from the German
by Michael Hamburger

Prodigy by Charles Simic,
drawings by Charles Seluzicki

Night of Shooting Stars by Leonardo Sinisgalli,
translated from the Italian by W. S. Di Piero

Skin by Tone Škrjanec,
translated from the Slovene by Matthew Rohrer and Ana Pepelnik

*We Women by Edith Södergran,
translated from the Swedish by Samuel Charters

Winterward by William Stafford

Baltics by Tomas Tranströmer
with photographs by Ann Charters,
translated from the Swedish by Samuel Charters

For the Living and the Dead by Tomas Tranströmer,
translated from the Swedish by John F. Deane

Prison by Tomas Tranströmer
with a postscript by Jonas Ellerström,
translated from the Swedish by Malena Mörling

Tomas Tranströmer's First Poems and
Notes From the Land of Lap Fever
by Tomas Tranströmer
with a commentary by Jonas Ellerström,
translated from the Swedish by Malena Mörling

Casual Ties by David Wevill

*Collected Poems by David Wevill

Collected Translations by David Wevill

Night is Simply a Shadow by Greta Wrolstad

Notes on Sea & Shore by Greta Wrolstad

The Countries We Live In by Natan Zach,
translated from the Hebrew by Peter Everwine

*forthcoming

Tavern Books is funded, in part, by the generosity of philanthropic organizations, public and private institutions, and individual donors. By supporting Tavern Books and its mission, you enable us to publish the most exciting poets from around the world. To learn more about underwriting Tavern Books titles, please contact us by e-mail: tavernbooks@gmail.com.

MAJOR FUNDING HAS BEEN PROVIDED BY

Lannan

The Libra Foundation

 Regional Arts & Culture Council

THE PUBLICATION OF THIS BOOK IS MADE POSSIBLE, IN PART, BY THE SUPPORT OF THE FOLLOWING INDIVIDUALS

Gabriel Boehmer
Dean & Karen Garyet
Mark Swartz & Jennifer Jones
The Mancini Family
Dorianne Laux & Joseph Millar
Pierre Rioux

Roby Roberts & Lael Pinney
Mary Ann Ryan
Marjorie Simon
Bill & Leah Stenson
Dan Wieden
Ron & Kathy Wrolstad

COLOPHON

This book was designed and typeset by Eldon Potter at Bryan Potter Design, Portland, Oregon. The text is set in Garamond, an old-style serif typeface named for the punch-cutter Claude Garamond (c. 1480-1561). Display font Raleway was designed in 2010 by Matt McInerney, and expanded into a 9-weight family by Pablo Impallari and Rodrigo Fuenzalida in 2012. Raleway is widely available through Google fonts. *Why We Live in the Dark Ages* appears in both paperback and cloth-covered editions. Printed on archival-quality paper by McNaughton & Gunn, Inc.